Almas Oskenbay

WordPress Start

Almas Oskenbay

WordPress Start

ScienciaScripts

Imprint
Any brand names and product names mentioned in this book are subject to trademark, brand or patent protection and are trademarks or registered trademarks of their respective holders. The use of brand names, product names, common names, trade names, product descriptions etc. even without a particular marking in this work is in no way to be construed to mean that such names may be regarded as unrestricted in respect of trademark and brand protection legislation and could thus be used by anyone.

Cover image: www.ingimage.com

This book is a translation from the original published under ISBN 978-620-6-15458-7.

Publisher:
Sciencia Scripts
is a trademark of
Dodo Books Indian Ocean Ltd. and OmniScriptum S.R.L publishing group

120 High Road, East Finchley, London, N2 9ED, United Kingdom
Str. Armeneasca 28/1, office 1, Chisinau MD-2012, Republic of Moldova, Europe
Printed at: see last page
ISBN: 978-620-6-01797-4

WORDPRESS
START

Training manual

UDC32.988.02-018
LBC 004.738.5
0-72

With the help of this tutorial, you can create internet resources yourself using the content management system WordPress. Thanks to its intuitive interface, the use of WordPress does not require knowledge of programming languages, which helps to develop the interests of the novice programmer.

The tutorial covers in sufficient detail the theoretical and practical issues involved in creating a website from start to finish. Students will learn how to register a domain name, select and purchase hosting, install and configure a content management system, select a design, install plug-ins, publish new content and manage the content of an Internet resource.

Table of Contents

CHAPTER 1. INTRODUCTION TO WORDPRESS

In this chapter, we'll explore what WordPress is made of and go through its main components, features and functions.

CONTENT MANAGEMENT SYSTEM

A content management system (CMS) is an information system or computer programme used to support and organise the collaborative process of creating, editing and managing content, otherwise known as content.

OPEN SOURCE

Open-source software is software that is open source. The source code of such software is available for review, study and change, which allows the user to make sure there are no vulnerabilities or unacceptable functions (e.g. hidden tracking of the program's user), to participate in improving the open software itself, to use the code to create new programs and correct errors in them - by borrowing the source code, if the license compatibility allows, or by studying the used algorithms, data structures, technologies, techniques and interfaces (as the source code can be used to create new programs).

RNR PROGRAMMING LANGUAGE

RNR (PHP: Hypertext Preprocessor; originally RNP/FI (Personal Home Page / Form Interpreter), later called Personal Home Page Tools) is a general-purpose scripting language used extensively for developing web applications. It is currently supported by the vast majority of web hosting providers and is one of the leaders among languages used to create dynamic websites.

The language and its interpreter (Zend Engine) are developed by a group of enthusiasts as an open source project. The project is distributed under its own licence[1] .

MYSQL

MySQL is a free relational database management system. MySQL is developed and maintained by Oracle Corporation, which acquired the trademark rights along with Sun Microsystems, which previously acquired the Swedish company MySQL AB. The product is distributed under both the GNU General Public License and its own commercial license. In addition, developers create functionality on demand for licensed users.

The flexibility of MySQL is due to its many table types: users can choose from MyISAM tables that support full-text search and InnoDB tables that support record-level transactions.

Furthermore, MySQL comes with a special EXAMPLE table type that demonstrates the principles of creating new table types. Thanks to the open architecture and GPL-licensing, new table types are constantly emerging in MySQL.

WHAT IS WORDPRESS?

WordPress is an open-source content management system. WordPress is written in the PHP programming language. It uses MySQL as the database server and is released under the GNU GPL version 2 license[2] . In short, it is free software that helps you create a beautiful website, blog or web application. Beautiful design, impressive features and the freedom to create whatever you want. WordPress can be used to create blogs to fairly sophisticated news resources. A built-in system of "themes and "plugins" together with a successful architecture allows you to construct projects of wide functional complexity.

Main functions:
- Customizable design;
- SEO-friendly;
- Adaptive mobile sites;
- High performance;
- Availability of a mobile app;
- High security;
- Flexible management of media files;
- Lightness and accessibility.

---

[2] 01 GNU General Public License (translated as 'GNU General Public License', 'GNU General Public License', or GNU Open Source License Agreement) is a free software license created by the GNU project in 1988 which assigns the software to the public domain. It is also called the GNU GPL for short, or even just the GPL.

You can extend the capabilities of WordPress with more than 55,000 plugins to make your site fit your needs. Options for adding an online shop, gallery, forum, analytics tools and more are provided.

<h3 align="center">OPPORTUNITIES</h3>

According to the community, more than 38% of all websites in the world run on WordPress, from personal blogs to major news outlets. More than 60 million people have already chosen WordPress for their internet 'home'.

WordPress combines simplicity for users and publishers. This makes it flexible, yet easy to use. Below is a list of some of the features that come standard with WordPress, however, there are thousands of plug-ins that extend the capabilities of WordPress, so the actual functionality is almost limitless. You're also free to write any code with WordPress, extending or modifying it in any way you like, or use it for commercial projects without any licensing fees. That's the beauty of free software, free doesn't just refer to the price, it's also free to have full control over it.

Here are some of the features you might like:

- Simplicity. Simplicity gives you the ability to go online and get publishing opportunities quickly. Nothing should prevent you from creating your website and putting content on it. WordPress is designed to make this happen.
- Flexibility. With WordPress, you can create any type of website: a personal blog or website, a photo blog, a business website, a professional portfolio, a government website, a magazine or news site, an online community, and even a network of websites. You can make your website beautiful with themes and add plugins. You can even create your own application.
- Publish with ease. If you've ever created a document, you're already a master of content creation with WordPress. You can create posts and pages, format them easily, insert multimedia, and with the click of a button, your content becomes live and posted online.
- Publishing tools. WordPress makes it easy for you to manage your content. Create drafts, schedule publishing and view corrections to your posts. Make your content public or private, and password protect posts and pages.
- User management. Not everyone needs the same access to your site. Administrators manage the site, editors handle the content, authors and contributors write that content, and subscribers have a profile that they can manage. This allows you to attract a wide variety of participants to

your website, while allowing others to simply be part of your community.

- Media management. Images can convey a thousand words, so it's important for you to be able to upload images and media to WordPress quickly and easily. Drag and drop media files into the upload tool to add them to your website. Add placeholder text and captions, and insert images and galleries into your content. A number of image editing tools are also available.

- Full standards compatibility. Every piece of code created by WordPress is fully compliant with the standards set by the W3C. This means your website will work on a modern browser, while maintaining direct compatibility with the next generation browser. Your website will be beautiful now and in the future.

- A simple design theme system. WordPress comes with three default themes, but if they're not for you, there's a theme directory with thousands of themes so you can create a beautiful website. None of them to your liking? Upload your own theme at the click of a button. You can completely change your website in seconds.

- Extension with plugins. WordPress comes with many features for every user. For every feature that isn't in the WordPress core, there's a plugin catalogue with thousands of plugins. Add sophisticated galleries, social networks, forums, social media widgets, spam protection, calendars, customise controls for search engine optimisation and forms.

- Embedded comments. Your blog is your home, and comments give your friends and subscribers the opportunity to interact with your content. WordPress' commenting tools give you everything you need to be a forum for discussion and moderation.

- Optimised for search engines. WordPress is optimised for search engines right out of the box. For more detailed SEO management, there are many SEO plugins that will take care of this for you.

- Use WordPress in your language. WordPress is available in more than 70 languages. If you or the person you're building the website for prefers to use WordPress in a language other than English, it's easy to do.

- Easy installation and updates. WordPress has always been and continues to be easy to install and update. Plenty of hosting providers offer one-click WordPress installation. Or, if you're comfortable, you can create a database and upload WordPress via FTP (or other convenient way) and run the installation.

- Import data. Using blogging or website software you don't like? Blogging on a hosted service that's about to close? WordPress comes

with import tools for Blogger, LiveJournal, Movable Type, TypePad, Tumblr and WordPress. If you're ready to make the move, we've made it easy for you.
- Freedom. WordPress is licensed under the GNU General Public License (GPLv2 or later), designed to protect your freedoms. You can use WordPress any way you want: install, use, modify, distribute. Software freedom is the foundation upon which WordPress is based.

WEBSITES CREATED WITH WORDPRESS

1. Clever Library for educators and parents - https://library.zti.kz
2. Linguistic Olympiads - https://wonder.zti.kz
3. Basic Elementary Education Olympiads - https://kokon.kz
4. Cyber Olympics in Italian draughts - https://doiby.zti.kz
5. Intellectual Cyber Chess Olympiads - https://chess.zti.kz
6. Competitions, conferences, olympiads - https://kzu.kz
7. National competitions, courses, conferences and olympiads - https://ukz.kz
8. Intellectual competitions, conferences and olympiads - https://tarim.kz
9. Methodological magazine for educators - https://adi&eme.kz
10. National distance competitions - http://clever.zti.kz
11. Competitions, conferences, olympiads - https://talimger.kz
12. International Olympiads - https://iae.su

CHAPTER 2. CHOOSING A DOMAIN NAME AND HOSTING

The very first step in creating your website is to choose a domain name. Although seemingly straightforward, there are some important points to be made about this task. In this chapter we offer answers to the obvious but popular questions. What do I need to know when choosing a domain name and hosting?

WHAT IS A DOMAIN?

A domain, or domain name, is an alphanumeric, numeric or alphanumeric designation that is a necessary element of a website address used on the Internet.

Domains are separated by hierarchy (levels):
- of the first (upper) level;
- second level;
- third level;
- etc.

Domain names below the third level are most often used for technical purposes. Example: clever.zti.kz
- kz - first level domain
- zti - second level domain
- clever - third level domain

Domain zones (first-level domains) are divided into two categories:

1. Geographical (national) domains, indicating whether a site belongs to a country or territory.

National domains are called ccTLDs - country code top-level domains. They are "tied" to a specific country. For example, .KZ, .RU, .US are geographical domains that are associated with Kazakhstan, Russia and the USA respectively.

2. General-purpose domains that are thematic.

General purpose domains are called gTLDs - generic top-level domains. They indicate the type of activity (theme) they belong to.

For example:
- .COM commercial - commerce;
- .NET network - network services;

- .BIZ business - international business.

Domain zones (second level domains)

Second-level domains contain an indication of the geographical location as well as the subject matter of the site. Examples of such "mixed" domain zones: .COM. KZ, .ORG.KZ.

.COM.KZ is commercial in Kazakhstan, .COM.RU is commercial in Russia, etc. Your domain in this zone will look like, for example, domain.com.kz.

Subdomains (subdomains)

These are domain names created within a primary domain. For example, you have registered the domain kzu.com. You can create sub-domains sub.kzu.com, subí. kzu.com, sub2.kzu.com. Within one domain you can create many subdomains. Most of the time the number of subdomains is limited by the specific hoster.

For second-level domain zones, it works in exactly the same way. For example, if you own the domain site.com.de, you can create subdomains poddomenl.site.com.de, poddomen2. site.com.de etc.

Subdomains are usually used in large companies that have diversified activities. For example, a holding company that includes several companies. Common domain holding.com, subdomain: companyl.holding.com, company2.holding.com etc.

Cyrillic domain zones

It is possible to register Cyrillic domain names in the zones. CLZ and .RF zones. For example: "domain.tsaz" , "best-domain.tsaz", etc. At the same time, there is an opinion that a Cyrillic domain is perceived by users as something less solid than a domain in English.

From a technical point of view, maintaining and configuring a Cyrillic domain is sometimes problematic due to incomplete software compatibility. As far as SEO is concerned, there are no problems with Cyrillic domains.

Hyphens in a domain name

Hyphens (a dash or minus sign) can be used in a domain name. Especially with a multi-word domain name, as spaces are not allowed. There is a restriction: spaces cannot be placed in place of the third and fourth characters of a domain, e.g. do- main.com. This applies to all domain names and registrars.

Reasons for restrictions

The restriction relates to domains that appear in the address bar in Cyrillic (or another alphabet) rather than Latin characters: mysite.tzaz, interestingsite.tzaz, etc.

For registrars, all alphabets except Latin are written in a special Punycode encoding and will look like this: xn-80arbjktj.xn-plag. In this encoding, hyphens on the third or fourth position are mandatory.

To avoid confusion and the misrepresentation of conventional domain names in Latin characters, the use of hyphens in domain names on the third and fourth character of the name is prohibited. On the other positions, hyphens can be used.

Criteria for selecting a domain

The name must be exclusive and not currently occupied. There cannot be two identical domain names in one domain zone, but can be in different zones, for example: sypersite.com, sypersite.ru, sypersite.net.

1. Think of a catchy name

1. Choose a domain name that is noble, memorable and easy to spell.

There are now hardly any free short second-level domain names of no more than 4 characters. Almost all of them are reserved, so it is not necessary to be guided by the principle "the shortest name possible".

2. Use a brand name in the domain name. Alternatively the brand name is a key query describing the company's activities. For example, "pokraska-mashini. by", "fa^-clining.ru".

3. Don't be afraid to use a few words (not long, 3-5 letters each).

4. Use abbreviations or acronyms if relevant to the topic of your website.

5. If the desired domain name is taken, try to buy back the domain you like from the current owner. Often domains are not used for websites, but are simply reserved and "parked" on some cheap hosting service. If a domain you like in your browser shows that it is "parked" it means that its owner is probably ready to sell it.

6. Do not use a consonant name with other brands, as this may confuse users.

Sometimes several variants are possible when translating a name from Cyrillic to Latin. For example, "powerful" is spelled as "moscni", "moshniy", "moschnij". To avoid confusion, avoid using such words in the name of the domain. Take into account that the letters Y, Y, Ch, Z, G, S,

T, Y are transcribed in several ways and it is better to avoid them in domain names in Latin characters.

2. Choose the right domain zone

For commercial regional resources, first check the national domain zone "linked" to the region where the buyers are located. Geo-referencing is important for search engine promotion.

For example, your shop delivers all over Kazakhstan, so your best option is the .kz domain zone. Working for Russia - .ru (Russia), etc.

The next highest priority are the second-level domain zones, com.kz, . org.kz etc. If the desired name is busy, check it in the topical domain zone, e.g. .org, .net, etc.

A website can be successful and have a good position in search engines by being in any domain zone, but it is not the optimal choice of domain zone:

- This will significantly increase the time it takes to promote your site in search engines. For example, if you trade in Kazakhstan and have chosen a generic domain, it will be more difficult for search engines to understand your geographical focus.
- Discourage customers. Users are more likely to trust sites that are in their domain zone. Kazakhstanis, for example, trust sites in the .com.kz and .kz domain zones more, while Russians trust sites in the .ru domain zone.

For commercial international resources

International websites should be registered in topical first-level domain zones. Geographic domain zones are not suitable in this case.

Information and non-profit resources

In the case of information resources, the choice of domain is not as important, as search engines and users are more focused on the language of the site.

A creative approach

Sometimes, most often in entertainment non-commercial topics, you can use homonymic domains. For example, you have a combination of domain name and domain zone that creates some additional meaning not obvious beforehand to your target audience: .NET (problem.net), .ME (lookat.me), .AM (whoi.am), etc.

3. Check the history of the domain

If the tenant of the domain does not renew the service, the domain is put up for sale and available for a new owner. Such domains are called "domains with a history".

This can be either positive or negative.

If a past site on this domain has been of good quality, it has been "looked after", the history of the site will be positive, and this will give the new tenant of the domain an extra edge in the search engines.

If there was a banned site (pornography, illegal goods, etc.) or if the site was hacked and spread viruses, the reputation of such a domain is poor (bad history).

Search engines are suspicious of sites on domains with a bad history. Promoting such a project can take a long time. The difference in promotion of a domain with a bad history compared to a domain with a positive history may be from a couple of months to a year.

To check domains for "history" you should use WHOIS services from domain registrars. This service is available at HOSTER.KZ and PS.KZ.

There is also a free service at https://whoisreque&.com/hi&ory/.

The service will show you everything that has happened to the site, what content has been posted there, etc. If you suspect that a domain has a negative history, don't take any chances.

WHAT DO I HAVE TO DO TO REGISTER A DOMAIN?

Domain prices and registration documents

When you register a domain name, you interact with the registrar company. When choosing a registrar, it is worth considering:
- the convenience of the register website;
- interactive prompts when searching for a free domain name.

This makes the selection process easier. Check the price of the desired domain from several registrars. Prices may differ for both registration and renewal. This is due to geographical affiliation and/or promotions for purchasing certain domains from the registrars the customer works with. For example, liosier.kz and ps.kz often have promotions on domain registration.

The domain registration process itself is not difficult. Personal details are entered on the registrar's website:
- NAME;

- email;
- phone number;
- mailing address.

Depending on the domain zone you have chosen, additional data and/or documents may be required.

For example:

- .ru zone - you will need to add a copy of your passport;
- .ia zone - a trademark corresponding to the name of the domain is required.

For example, to register a domain name goodday.ua, you must be the owner of the trademark goodday and have supporting documents.

Once you have selected a domain zone, carefully read the registration rules. For example, to register a .sot topical domain, according to the rules of the domain zone, you do not need to provide documents. And if the registrar requires documents, it is the registrar's own rule and it may not be worth cooperating with it.

Algorithm of action when registering a domain

1. Come up with a domain name.
2. Choose a domain name registrar company.
3. Check whether the selected domain name is available for registration. Most domain registrars have special tools for this.
4. If the domain is available for registration, you can place an order and pay for it. Once payment has been received by the registrar, the domain is taken over by the customer.
5. When you receive the domain under management, delegate it to the DNS servers. The DNS service[3] is either provided by the domain registrar itself or by your hosting company.

A tool to check the availability of a domain on the PS Internet Company website.

Note that you can register a domain with one company and host a website with another. There are no difficulties in setting up the domain or breaking the registration rules.

We recommend using the services of the domain registrar PS Internet Company. The company provides hosting services for websites of any complexity, registers domains in 400 zones and offers its clients

---

[3] *01 DNS is a special service which binds a domain name to specific IP addresses through which communication on the Internet takes place. Without binding (delegation) to DNS, a domain name is useless and cannot be used to operate a website.*

technical support 24/7 without holidays and weekends. They will help you choose the best hosting option for your website.

HOW TO CHOOSE A HOSTING SERVICE?

The question of choosing the right hosting for your website is important for any webmaster. Of course, in recent years there are alternatives in the form of website builders, but to create modern dynamic, focused on interaction with visitors to web-projects, their capabilities are not enough due to limitations on connecting scripts and lack of support for RNR as the most popular programming language for web-development.

When a user starts to select hosting for their project, they are confronted with an abundance of terms, technical characteristics, pricing plans and features of different platforms. If we choose by rational criteria, we must first answer the question: how much should we pay for hosting, and whether we should pay at all?

Paid or free hosting?
It's a truism that a miser pays twice. But almost all of today's Internet is geared towards free services:
- free document maintenance in Google Docs;
- free creation of layouts and designs in Figma;
- free website builders;
- etc.

If you think about it, it is easy to conclude that the engine of free services on the Internet is advertising. Free hostings usually embed their ad units in the sites they host. Whether the site owner needs it is up to him.

Stability and usability of services provided is also not a strong point of free hosting. Most likely, a modern dynamic website will work on such hosting is extremely slow and will be able to serve a minimal number of visitors. For a simple static information page, such hosting may be suitable.

The resource limits of free hosting companies are as limited as possible. Many simply do not have support for PHP scripts and the ability to connect to the database, sending email. Thus, these hosts are suitable only for the simplest sites consisting of static pages.

A special mention should be made of the free trial periods offered by hosting providers to demonstrate their services. When selecting such a tariff, the user receives for a certain period of time, usually not less than a week, the entire range of services of the provider, almost similar to its commercial tariffs. This is the best way to get acquainted with the features and functionality and to assess the stability and convenience of the service.

Free testing of PS Internet Company hosting.

You can test the operation of the hosting service during a free 7-day period. Which services have a test period?

- Virtual hosting for private individuals and companies - booked via a private office, instructions are on the company's website.
- Virtual hosting for 1C-Bitrix - to be ordered through your personal account, instructions are on the company's website.
  - VPS (Virtual Private Server) - arranged through the sales department.

ISPMANAGER WEB HOSTING CONTROL PANEL

ISPmanager is a commercial web hosting control panel which allows you to manage software such as web server (Apache/Nginx), database server (MySQL/Po&greSQL), mail server (Sendmail/Exim/Po&fix) and other related software via a web interface.

The main features are the operation with a standard software configuration, which is installed from the operating system repository, the availability of localisation in several languages, the support of AP1-interface[4] .

ISPmanager tops the list of the most popular hosting control panels used by web studios and internet agencies in Kazakhstan, according to an independent study by the Institute of Intelligent Technologies.

ISPmanager Lite provides site owners with a rich set of tools to manage their web-server: create an unlimited number of users, sites, domains, etc. ISPmanager Lite is integrated with website builders, anti-viruses, Let's Encrypt, etc.

Features of ISPmanager:
- Configuring Apache and Nginx web servers
- CMS installation and website creation
- Setting up domains and DNS records
- Alternative versions of RNR
- File manager
- Backup

---

4 01 The acronym API stands for Application ProgrammingInterface (API). It is a description of the ways (a set of classes, procedures, functions, structures or constants) that one computer program can communicate with another program

- Working with databases
- Security
- Hosting with ISPmanager Business

ISPmanager Lite provides a rich set of tools to manage the server - create an unlimited number of sites, domains, email addresses, users, etc. The panel is suitable for both virtual and dedicated servers.

Through ISPmanager you can install the popular content management system (CMS) WordPress on your web-server. Users of ISPmanager can install alternative versions of RNR[5] - from 5.2 to 7.1. This allows different RNR versions to be hosted on one server. The RNR version of PHP PHP is usually installed in the server operating system. If you try to host several PHP versions, they may not work correctly. ISPmanager helps to correct this problem.

Alternative versions of RNR in ISPmanager can be used for all RNR modes:

- as CGI;
- as an Apache module;
- as Fa&CGI (PHP-lpm);
- as Fa&CGI (an Apache module).

---

[5] 01 Alternate versions of RNR are binary files and Apache modphp modules. which ISPsysíem builds and updates regularly. They are included in the boxed version of ISPmanager and allow you to install a separate version of RNR for each site.

CHAPTER 3. INSTALLING AND SETTING UP WORDPRESS

In this chapter we'll look at installing WordPress in 5 minutes and take a closer look at all the information about the process.

INSTALLATION PREPARATION

WordPress is well known for its easy installation. In most situations, installing WordPress is a very simple process and takes less than five minutes from start to finish. Many web hosts offer tools (e.g. internet company PS[6]) to install WordPress automatically. However, if you want to install WordPress yourself, the following guide will help. And with automatic updates, it's even easier. But, there are a few things you'll need to know before you start the installation.

You need access to your site, its directories and software for the installation process. This:
- Access to your site (shell or FTP)
- Text editor
- FTP client (if you are installing WordPress on a remote server)
- The browser you are using.

Start the installation with:
- Checks your server to ensure it meets the minimum requirements of WordPress.
- Getting the latest version of WordPress.
- Unzip the resulting file into a folder on your computer.

WORDPRESS INSTALLATION

Below are brief instructions, for those who are already familiar with the process of installing various web applications.

1. Download and unpack the WordPress distribution package if you haven't already done so.
2. Create a database for WordPress on your web server so that your MySQL user has full rights to access and make changes to it.
3. Rename the wp-config-sample.php file to wp-config.php.
4. Open wp-config.php in your favourite text editor and type in the database connection settings.

[6] O1 Provides website hosting services for websites of any complexity, registers domains in 400 zones and offers its customers 24/7 technical support with no holidays and weekends.

5. Place the files on a recognisable web server:

- If you want to install WordPress in the root of your site (e.g. http://example.com/), move all the contents of the pre-unpacked WordPress distribution to the root folder of the web server.

- If you want to install WordPress in a separate folder on your webserver (e.g. http://example.com/blog/), rename the wordpress folder to the name of the folder where you want to install the system and move it to the webserver. For example, if you want to install WordPress in the "blog" folder on the web server, then you would need to rename the "wordpress" folder to "blog" and move it to the root of the web server.
  6. Go to wp-admin/in&all.php using your web browser.
- If you have installed WordPress in the root of the web server, go to: http:// example.com/wp-admin/in&all.php
- If you have installed WordPress in the actual folder you created on the webserver, e.g. blog, then go to: http://example.com/blog/wp-admin/in&all.php

That's it! If you have done everything correctly, the installation of WordPress is successfully completed.

INSTALLATION IN DETAIL

Step 1: Loading and unpacking

Download and unpack the WordPress distribution by going to http://ru. wordpress.org/releases/.
1. If you will be installing WordPress on a remote web server, download and extract the WordPress distribution to your computer using your favourite web browser.
2. If you have shell access to a web server and experience with console applications, you can upload WordPress directly to a web server using wget[7] (lynx or other console mode software) to avoid incomplete downloads when FTPing internet connections are slow:
    - wget http://wordpress.org/late&.tar.gz
    - Unpack the distribution using: tar -xzvflate&.tar.gz

The WordPress distribution will be unpacked to a folder called wordpress in the same folder (directory) where you downloaded the

---

[7] 01 Wget is a free, non-interactive console program for downloading files over the network. It supports the HTTP, FTP and HTTPS protocols and also supports operation through an HTTP proxy server. It is included in almost all GNU/Linux distributions. Wgetemc is a non-interactive program.

late&.tar.gz archive.

3. If you don't have shell access to a web server or experience with console applications, you can upload WordPress directly to a web server using ZipDeploy.

Step 2: Creating the database and user

If you're using a hosting provider, you may already have a pre-installed database for WordPress, or your hosting provider provides automatic database creation. Contact your hosting provider's support team or use the cPanel hosting control panel to find out all the details about creating a database and getting users up and running.

If you still need to create the database and user yourself, please refer to the instructions below: Accessing phpMyAdmin on Different Servers, Working with Plesk instructions[8] or Working with phpMyAdmin[9] .

If you are installing WordPress on your own web server, refer to the instructions in Working with phpMyAdmin or Working with MySQL Client to create the database and user to install WordPress.

Working with Plesk

If your hosting provider uses Plesk, you can use the instructions below to create the database and user to subsequently install WordPress.

1. Log in to Plesk.
2. Click the MySQL Databases link.
3. If you don't have a user for WordPress among the Users list, create one:
- Select a user for WordPress (e.g. 'wordpress') and enter its name in the UserName field.
- Select a password (preferably including upper and lower case characters, special characters, numbers and letters) and enter it in the Password field.
    - Select the user name and password you have just created.
    - Click Add User.
4. If you don't have a database for WordPress in the Databases list, get

---

[8] *01 Plesk is a commercial web hosting platform. The Plesk control panel allows the server administrator to create new websites, reseller accounts, email accounts and DNS records using a web interface.*

[9] *02phpMyAdmin is an open-source web application written in PHP and is a web interface for MySQL DBMS administration. PhpMyAdmin allows you to administer MySQL server, run SQL commands and view the contents of tables and databases through a browser and beyond.*

one:

- Select a name for the WordPress database (e.g. 'wordpress' or 'blog') and
  enter it in the Db field, click Add Db.

5. In the Databases field, select the username for the WordPress
Database using the User drop-down list, then select the database from the
Db drop-down list. Check all the checkboxes in the Privileges field and
then click Add User to Db.

```
$
$   $dbh = mysql_connect(«hostname», «username», «<PASSWORD HERE>») or die
    («message»);
$   mysql_select_db(«databasename»);
$
```

6. When you return to the main MySQL Account Properties window,
   Plesk will display the information about the database you just created.
   You should see the username you just attached to the database (with
   ALL PRIVILEGES ticked), and additional information on Connection
   settings to use Perl or RNR scripts to connect to the database. The RNP
   code will be as follows:

Change the hostname, username, databasename and the password
you chose. (Note the hostname field should in most cases be set to
localho&.)

Working with phpMyAdmin

If you have phpMyAdmin installed on your web server, follow the
instructions below to create the database and user for the subsequent
installation of WordPress.
Note: These instructions are for phpMyAdmin version 2.6.0; therefore the
appearance of phpMyAdmin may differ from the phpMyAdmin installed
on your web server.
1. If the database to install WordPress has not yet been created in the
   Database drop-down menu on the left, then create it:
- Choose a database name for WordPress (e.g. 'wordpress' or 'blog'), enter
  it in the Create new database field and click Create.
2. Click on the Note icon in the top left corner of the window to return to
   the main software page, then click Privileges. If the user is not already
   created for a WordPress installation, create one:
    - Click Add a new User.
- Select a username for WordPress (e.g. 'wordpress') and enter it in the
  User name field. (Make sure the Use text field: is selected in the drop-

down list.)

  •   Select a password (preferably one that includes the characters before

  •   (Make sure the Use text field: is selected in the drop-down list and re-enter the password in the Re-type field. (Ensure that the Use text field: is selected in the drop-down list.) Re-type the password in the Re-type field.

  • Make a note of the user name and password you have just created.

  • Leave all Global privileges list options unchanged.

  • Press Go.

3. Go back to the Privileges tab and click on theCycle privileges icon associated with your user for WordPress. In the Database-specific privileges section, select the database you just created for WordPress and select Add privileges to the following database from the drop-down list. The page will reload and change the user's privileges automatically for the selected database. Click Check All to double check all user privileges and click Go.

4. On the report page, note the server name that comes after the Server: entry at the top of the page. (Most of the time it is localho^.)

Working with the MySQL client

If you have shell access to the web server, are comfortable using the command line, and your MySQL user has permissions to create other MySQL users and databases, then you can use the instructions below to create a user and database for WordPress.

```
$
$  mysql -u adminusername -p
Enter password:
Welcome to the MySQL monitor.  Commands end with ; or \g.
Your MySQL connection id is 5340 to server version: 3.23.54

Type 'help;' or '\h' for help. Type '\c' to clear the buffer.

mysql> CREATE DATABASE databasename;
Query OK, 1 row affected (0.00 sec)

mysql> GRANT ALL PRIVILEGES ON databasename.* TO
«wordpressusername»@»hostname»
  -> IDENTIFIED BY «password»;
Query OK, 0 rows affected (0.00 sec)

mysql> FLUSH PRIVILEGES;
Query OK, 0 rows affected (0.01 sec)
```

```
mysql> EXIT
Bye
$
```

Explanation:

- adminusemame is most often set to root, unless you have another account with higher privileges.
- wordpress or blog are appropriate names for your databasename.
- wordpress a suitable name for the username wordpressusemame.
- hostname is usually set to localliost. If you do not know the value of this variable, you are advised to check it with your system administrator.
- password - preferably include upper and lower case characters, special characters, numbers and letters.

Write the values you use for the variables databasename, wordpressusemame, hostname. and password.

Step 3: Configuring the wp-config.php file

Note: This step can be skipped. File wp-config.php can be created automatically (if the webserver process has write permissions to the installation folder) simply by accessing your site, you will only need to enter the database server address, database user name, database name, table prefix and administrator account name and password for it. That's all! Or you can continue reading below to find out how to set up wp-config.php manually.

In this part, all changes are made to the next part of the code:

```
// ** MySQL settings ** //
define('DB_NAME', 'putyourdbnamehere');    // Имя базы данных
define('DB_USER', 'usernamehere');    // Имя пользователя MySQL
define('DB_PASSWORD', 'yourpasswordhere'); // ...и пароль
define('DB_HOST', 'localhost');    // 99% что вам не следует вносить изменения в данную строчку кода
define('DB_CHARSET', 'utf8');
define('DB_COLLATE', '');
```

1. Going back to Step 1 where you unpacked the distribution with WordPress, rename the wp-config-sample.php file to wp-config.php.

2. Open the renamed wp-config.php file with your favourite text editor and make changes according to the example code above:

   DB_NAME (Name of the database created for WordPress in Step 2).
   DB_USER (User name for WordPress in Step 2).
DB_PASSWORD (The password you selected for the user in WordPress in Step 2).
DB_HOST (The hostname you found out in Step 2 (usually localliosE but not always).
DB_CHARSET (Database encoding, in most cases does not need to be changed.) DB_COLLATE (Database check, in most cases the value does not need to be changed and is left blank. See Editing wp-config.php for more details).

3. Save the file.

Step 4: Placing files

Now you need to decide exactly where you want your WordPress blog to be located on your website:
• In the root directory of your website. (For example, http://example.com/)
• In a subdirectory (subdirectory) on your website. (For example, http://example. com/blog/)

Note: The location of the root directory in the file system on your web server may vary considerably depending on your hosting provider and the software they use. Check with your hosting provider or system administrator for the exact location of the root directory.

Placing files in the root directory
- If you want to host the files on a web server - use your favourite FTP client to upload the entire contents of the wordpress folder (but not the folder itself) to the web server's root directory.
- If the files are already located on the web server and you use shell access to install WordPress, move the entire contents of the wordpress folder (but not the folder itself) to the root directory of the web server.

Placing files in a subdirectory
- If you want to host the files on a web server, then rename the wordpress folder with the desired name, then using your favourite FTP client, upload the folder to the root directory of the web server.
- If the files are already located on the web server and you are using shell access to install WordPress, transfer the entire contents of the wordpress folder to the web server to a folder you have previously created with the desired name, which is located in the root directory.

Step 5: Starting the installation
Launch your favourite web browser to start the installation.

- If you have placed the WordPress files in the root directory of the web server, then go to: http://example.com/wp-admin/in&all.php
- If you have placed the WordPress files in a subdirectory named blog, for example, go to: http://example.com/blog/wp-admin/in&all.php

Please note that during installation you will be asked to enter the name of your future Weblog and your email address. You can also check the box for "show my Weblog on search engines" if you don't mind your blog being indexed by search engines. You can choose not to check this box, in which case your blog will be accessible to users, but search engines will not index your blog. Note that all the information you have entered at this stage of the installation can be further modified in the Admin Panel.

Solving problems when starting the installation
In case you receive a database-related error message during the installation process:
- Go back to Step 2 and Step 3, and check that the database and user data you previously created is correct in the wp- config.php file.
- Make sure that the user you created earlier has full access rights to the

WordPress database Step 3.
- Ensure that the server required to run the database is up and running.

COMMON INSTALLATION PROBLEMS

The following describes common problems encountered during the installation of the system. For more detailed information and solutions to problems with installing WordPress, refer to the Installation Guide and the Troubleshooting Guide.

I see a lot of errors Headers already sent. How can I fix it?
- You may have made a mistake when editing wp-config.php.
- Download wp-config.php (if you have access to the shell).
- Open it in your favourite text editor.
- Make sure that the first line contains nothing but <?php and that there are NO text, spaces or blank lines before it.
- Make sure that the last line contains nothing but ?> and that there are NO text, spaces or blank lines after it.
- Save the file, upload it again if necessary, and refresh the page in your browser.

At the beginning of installation, the error "Cannot modify header information - headers already sent by (output Parted at C:\xampp\htdocs\wordpress\wp-config.php:1) in ..." often appears. Open the wp-config.php file with a text editor such as notepad. Select "Save file as..." and choose ANSI coding instead of UNICODE or UTF. Refresh the page.

There are a lot of "<?php?>" tags on the page.
- If the <? Php?> tags are visible in the browser, it means that your PHP is not working properly. All PHP code must be executed before the server sends the resulting HTML code to your web browser. (That's why it's called a preprocessor.) Make sure your web server meets the requirements to run WordPress, that the RNR is installed and properly configured, or ask your hosting provider or system administrator for help-

I keep getting an error message when connecting to the database, but I'm sure my configuration is correct.
- Try resetting MySQL password manually. If you have access to MySQL via the shell, try entering it:

```
SET PASSWORD FOR 'wordpressusername'@'hostname' = OLD_
PASSWORD('password');
```

- If you are using MySQL version before 4.1, use PASSWORD instead of OLD_PASSWORD. If you don't have shell access, you can simply enter the above in a SQL query in phpMyAdmin. Otherwise you may need to use your host's control panel to reset the password for your database user.

Uploaded images and audio files do not work.

- If you use the Rich Text Editor on a blog that is installed in a subdirectory and drag and drop a newly uploaded image into the editor box, the image may disappear after a couple of seconds. This is because TinyMCE (the Rich Text Editor) does not get enough information during the drag and drop operation to correctly build a path to the image or other file. The solution is not to drag and drop uploaded images into the editor. Instead, press and hold the image and select "Send to Editor".

How to recover the WordPress admin password

- Log in to phpMyAdmin. The database access details are in the wp-config.php file and click on your site's database.
- In the list of tables, click on the wp_users table. The prefixes can have different values.
  - On the line with user_login "admin" press "Change".
- In the window that opens, select the MD5 function from the drop-down list in the user_pass line, and enter the new administrator password in the next window. Remember or make a note of the new password - this is used to log in to the CMS admin area. Then click Next at the bottom of the page. Done. You've successfully changed your WordPress admin password.

Which password is considered secure?

Set a strong password for WordPress so that you don't lose control of your site if there is a risk of it being compromised. For maximum security when creating a passphrase, it is recommended that you

- Include uppercase and lowercase letters, numbers and symbols.
- Avoid meaningful words, birthdates or other combinations that can be easily guessed.

Like many web applications, WordPress stores all user accounts in a MySQL database. For security purposes, passwords are encrypted in the database. In the case of WordPress, they are processed using an MD5 cryptographic hash algorithm. It converts any string into a jumble of letters and symbols that is nearly impossible to recover into the original passphrase.

CHAPTER 4. WORKING WITH WORDPRESS CONTENT

Posts and pages in WordPress are almost identical and at the same time completely different ways of publishing content on your website.

Both entries and pages have the same interface for publishing in the WordPress admin. They have the same sets of attributes, but they're still different. Let's figure out what's what!

RECORDS

Entries (or posts) are a data type that are linked to the date of publication, sorted in reverse chronological order (new items at the top, others on subsequent pages), and are generally displayed on your home page.

In short, entries are what make a website a blog.

Records are used to publish news, instructions, articles, reviews, reports on a regular basis. In general, whatever you want and what happens at a particular point in time.

A key feature of entries is that they are time-based. It is this feature that allows search engines to see that your site is alive rather than "dead". The more often the content appears on the site, the more your site is liked by Google, Yandex or any other search engine. The date is displayed in the search results and the user can immediately understand whether the material is relevant to him or her, or whether it is already obsolete.

Entries have a set of attributes specific to them: date of publication, heading, tag, author, format and a number of other minor attributes. All of these properties can be used to structure your site: you can view entries for a specific date, heading or tag, author or format of the publication you want.

Each of the entry properties can be used when displaying on the home page or a dedicated blog page. For example, you can show only the "News" column on the home page, or a specific author, or only for that week. To put it simply, you have much more flexibility in how you display your content.

What you can do with records in WordPress:
- Link to one or more headings;
- Assign any number of labels to link to other themed entries;
- Allow other users to add content to your website;

- Change the design of entries depending on the format used, if your theme supports this;
  - Set up automatic BRSS broadcasting;
- Set up automatic posting to social media or to your newsletter by your blog's subscribers.

What you can't do with records:
  - You can't display the entry as the home page of the website;
  - You cannot make one record a child of another.

PAGE

Pages in WordPress are used to create static content that is in no way tied to the author who published it or to the date. The implication is that pages are created once and will not be updated regularly.

You can form the pages into a hierarchical structure, thereby showing the dependency of one on the other. For example, you have a Services page, which includes the pages "Design development", "Search engine promotion". Or you have "Hot Dishes" and it has pages like "Chicken", "Beef" and so on. Each sub-page is designed as a drop-down menu below its parent page.

Typical examples of pages on many websites: "About the author", "Contacts", "Reviews". Any of the pages in WordPress can be made the main page, and then it will appear as the very first page when you enter your site.

Almost always pages are used to form the main menu on the site - any of the items refer to a static page rather than to a specific entry or heading. WordPress makes it possible to do otherwise.

If you want to make a particular page the home page and don't want to give up publishing entries, then you'll have to create a second page and name it "Blog" or "News", for example, and then specify in the WordPress settings that this page will be used to display your posts.

Each page can be uniquely designed independently of the content on it. For example, the contact page may be full-width without a sidebar, while the home page will be full-width and have a sidebar for widgets. It all depends on the capabilities of your theme.

CONTENT MANAGEMENT

Content is exactly what people go to your blog or website for from search engines. The higher quality content on pages and posts, the more accurately they answer users' questions, the better for everyone.

Content preparation is also a job not to be forgotten. In this section, we'll look at working with you on all types of content: text, images, video, integration with third-party sites.

How to insert a YouTube video into WordPress

It's very common when blogging to add videos from YouTube to a post or page. I see no reason why you shouldn't use this service when posting your videos online. I will list just a few of them that keep me hooked on this service.

YouTube for bloggers is handy for everything:
- The most famous and supported by all browsers;
- When working with video, you can add the effects you need;
- Supports video quality up to 4K;
- Works on all mobile platforms;
- Easy to integrate into many popular CMS using plugins or iframes;
- It has a good affiliate programme.

In this tutorial we'll look at two ways to add YouTube videos to your website.

Using oEmbed technology

The YouTube service is on the list of sites that support oEmbed technology, which means that you can simply copy the link from the address bar of your browser and paste it into the text input form in WordPress.

Take the desired video, copy the link from your browser's address bar and simply paste it into the editor's visual mode directly into the text. Before you know it, the link is automatically transformed into a video. This feature has been around for a while, but it's in video preview mode - in the latest WordPress update.

The only inconvenience here is that you won't be able to set the size of the video and it will be a different size every time. This will probably depend on the maximum possible size of the video itself, or maybe something else.

Inserting YouTube videos via HTML code

On the YouTube screen, find the controls below the video and go to "Share". You'll immediately have the code to embed the video on your website. Almost always the most popular size is 960 pixels wide, which fits most websites because it displays optimally on both desktop and mobile browsers. But more often than not, you have to resize it to fit your site, as the width of the text area varies from site to site.

Warning! If you insert the video in a visual editor, then the HTML code of your video will be converted in such a way that the video will not work on your website. I therefore strongly recommend switching to "Text" mode so that the video will display correctly on your site when inserted in the second way.

Using headings

A rubric is a feature of an entry that allows you to structure material around different topics. For example, if you are blogging about travel, then each country is a rubric.

A typical example of the use of headings is the sections in this training manual. Each instruction belongs to a different category of material. And all together they will make up the structure of the information resource.

You can almost instantly find the instructions you are looking for, simply because there is a list of headings on the left that makes it clear what is in them.

You can create a heading via the menu or the "Headings" widget. You can delete an unneeded rubric in the table view by first ticking the rubric and then selecting "Delete" from the "Actions" menu.

Rubrics are deleted instantly and cannot be recovered. There is no recycle bin (as in records and pages).

Using labels

Labels allow you to group entries from different categories by a common attribute. The fundamental difference between labels and headings is that labels cannot be nested. It is a simple "flat" list, unlike the tree-like structure of headings.

The headings could be: first course, second course, barbecue, drinks, aperitifs, that sort of thing. And the tags are the types of food. For example, "potato dishes", "no carbohydrates", "no sugar", "meat". That is, for each post about a dish, you can attach labels that categorise it.

Image editor

WordPress has some simple image editing features in its arsenal. It's not Adobe Photoshop or similar, of course, but you can change the size or orientation.

WordPress text editor modes

The main tool for working on content in WordPress is the text editor. This is used to fill the site with content, writing, formatting and other things.

Don't expect to get all the power of Microsoft Word in your browser, and I would advise against this misconception. But you can design the text, add images, videos, right/left alignment, or whatever else you want, without any problem.

How do I set a password for a page or entry in WordPress?

In WordPress, it is possible to restrict access to any page or entry by setting a password. Only those users to whom you give the password will have read access. The rest of us will just see the password form.

How do I make a static home page?

With each passing year, WordPress is increasingly moving away from the "blogging engine" label in favour of business websites, online shops and one-page sites. The demands of users are also changing.

The first thing business site owners want is a static home page, because it is the first page that tells the visitor about the company, its services and allows them to continue to get to know each other.

Many premium themes (which are bought for money) have their own mechanism for customising the homepage and the material in this manual may not be useful. Please keep this in mind.

By default, WordPress displays the last N posts on the home page in reverse chronological order. It's a common blog format, nothing unusual and you're already familiar with it.

This behaviour is almost always used in most free themes. With only a few exceptions, free themes may make the home page a static page instead of a blog.

This tutorial will only be necessary for those who, after installing the theme, display posts on the home page, rather than sliders, service boxes and other non-blog elements.

Creating pages

In order to set up a static home page, it must first be created. Go to menu "Pages" - "Add new", type in the desired text and publish it.

Here's the tricky part: since you and I are removing the blog posts from the home page, we have yet to create a separate page called "Blog", for example. This will be used to display your entries.

All in all, after these operations you will have two pages: "Home" and "Blog", you can choose the shortcut yourself. We recommend using "home" or "blog", simple and straightforward.

Installing the home page

Now it's only a matter of time before we mark our newly created page as the home page. To do this, go to "Settings" - "Reading" and set the settings box we are interested in. Switch the option to "Static page" and you are given the opportunity to select from a list of pages the newly created new pages.Save and go to the home page, making sure that instead of records, it is now the information you need about your company or project.

In fact, you don't need to create a homepage specifically, but can use one of the existing pages, such as About or Services. This is the best option for a business website.

For a blog, this could be a welcome page, or a page about the author. But you can also modify the template so that both the posts on the home page and the desired greeting are visible.

If you have created a page to display blog entries, you will need to add a link to it in the main menu, otherwise the user simply won't be able to find it.

WordPress, programming languages and database management tools are improving day by day. So in this tutorial we have tried to give just the basics for getting started and a general understanding.

CHAPTER 5. WEBSITE DESIGN

Website design is the visual design of the pages, the combination of all its graphic elements. In this chapter we will try to talk about the importance of website design: what it consists of, what are the stages involved in creating websites and who it is better to contact for design.

Why do I need a website design?

Talking about what website design is from an entrepreneur's point of view, let's say that it is needed for the convenience of visitors. When designing, a lot of attention is paid to the arrangement of content, the choice of trust triggers and grip elements. The design of a company's website accentuates the right elements. A good design creates the right image for the company.

What does website design consist of?

To create a great website design, you need to decide on the structure, the blocks and the customer's wishes. Knowing trends and analysing competitors' sites can help you make the right decision.

What goes into a website design:
- Photos showing your product or interaction with it.
- Icons for lists.
- Graphic elements.
- Different fonts.
- Brand colours.
- Logo.

The software code, trust triggers and text are not components of the website design.

It is up to the doer to decide what to do with the website design. It is not so much the tool that matters, but the result. The most popular programmes are: Sketch, Adobe XD, Figma, InVision Studio, Webflow, Adobe PhotoShop, Corell Draw, etc.

What is adaptive website design?

Adaptive web design ensures that web pages display correctly on most gadgets. The design adapts to the size of devices.

There is also a mobile version of the website. It is developed separately, putting some of the information from the main version. The mobile site has its own address, too. The mobile version has a link to the main site.

Why does a website need a design concept?

A designer needs to think about how to design a website and whether it will be profitable. The website concept will determine what the site will be like, what its purpose is and how it differs from the competition. Without this step, it is impossible to build a marketing strategy.

The main thing to consider when designing a website is for whom it is being created. The client must provide information about the customers, their tastes and typical behaviour on the internet. Otherwise, the website will not be profitable.

How to create a beautiful website?

For a commercial website, it is not beauty that is important, but the exact fit with the user's needs. There are four components to creating a website:

1. Visual design. The website should be clear and user-friendly. You should not use flashy objects, such as animations, flash banners or other complex attributes, as it is difficult to ensure that they display correctly on all devices. Good website design in 2022 does not distract the customer.
2. Design exclusivity. It is important that the design communicates your brand, is memorable and leaves a pleasant aftertaste.
3. Keeping up to date with today's demands. Understand trends on Awwwards, Behance, Pinterest. Make selections, analyse the appeal of the sites. Ask the right questions. Why do I like this particular site? How do the different elements work for the audience? Write down recurring elements in the best designs.
4. Testing on the target audience. After launching the website, you need to assess how the target audience responds to it. Are users not confused by the navigation? Do they click on the links? Do they go to other sections?

4 stages of website design

The stages are similar to a 'website creation' service: from discussing the job to handing over the project.

1. Writing the terms of reference. This is where website design starts.

After sending the application, the designer discusses the project with the client. The contractor uses the brief[10] to clarify all questions.

- Is there a logo and corporate identity for the website? If yes, ask for a vector format to be sent to[11] .
- Any requests for colours? For colour matching you can use https://color.adobe.com/en/explore
    - Any sites you like? 1st place, 2nd place, 3rd place ...
    - Are there sites that you categorically dislike?
    - What was wrong with the old site?
    - Which target audience is the website aimed at?
    - What area will the site cover?
    - Social media links.

2. Site prototype. This is a schematic representation of the blocks on the page. The prototype shows the preliminary structure of the site. It can be made as an html or other template at the client's request. The purpose of the prototype is to understand what the site will be like, so as not to make any mistakes before launching it. It is the foundation of the site.
3. A website layout is a graphical layout with indentation, shading and other parameters in static form. PSD[12] website mock-ups are needed to assess visual flaws in the first stages of work, to demonstrate design ideas, to assist the programmer, to get visions of the site and customer approval. As a result PSD mockup forms a concept of the site for the designer, client, marketer and programmer. Each specialist must be satisfied with the mock-up. Then the website design will be developed quickly and clearly.
4. Structuring the site. The team decides what the home page and the rest of the site will look like. Each element, its scope and importance on the page are important. The entire structure of the site is aimed at making the visitor feel comfortable and selling the company's product.

Website design on WordPress

We've been through the basics of website design. Now let's take a look at what WordPress has to offer!

WordPress contains millions of ready-made themes that you can use

---

[10] 01 A Brief is a document in which the client and the contractor define tasks, clarify upcoming work steps and discuss possible technical details in order to quickly create a common context that is clear to all parties and to be on the same page for the project.

[11] 01 Vector format is a higher stage of image manipulation. This type of image consists of vectors, infinite curves, which allows for high clarity at all scales.

[12] 02 PSD - Raster format for storing graphic information, used in Adobe Photoshop.

to build a website for your project. You'll find themes that are lightweight and highly extensible. There are also versatile themes whose functionality will allow you to build almost any type of website: a blog, a portfolio, a business website and an online shop on WooCommerce[13] with a beautiful and professional design.

Find a quick and easy theme for yourself, adaptive and ready to translate. Modern themes are structured with SEO best practices[14], unique WooCommerce features to increase conversions[15]. You'll be able to change the settings on tablets and smartphones so that your website will look great on any device. Most of the premium themes are now compatible with the most popular page builders, such as Elementor, Beaver Builder, Visual Composer, Divi, SiteOrigin, etc. Developers will love the extensibility of the code, turning this into a nice customisation and tweaking experience.

---

[13] 01 *WooCommerce is the world's most popular open-sourceonline shopping platform.*

[14] 02 *SEO (Search Engine Optimisation) is a set of measures to improve a website's ranking in search engines.*

[15] 03 *Conversion in internet marketing is the ratio of the number of visitors who have taken targeted actions (hidden or direct instructions from advertisers, merchants or contentcreators - purchase, register, subscribe, visit a specific page, click on an ad link) to the total number of visitors to the website, expressed as a percentage. For example: you have an online shop selling some products. Suppose that 500 unique visitors come to it every day. During those days there are 7 different purchases in your shop. To find the conversion rate, divide the number of purchases by the number of visitors: 7/500 = 0.014 = 1.4 per cent.*

CHAPTER 6. WORKING WITH WORDPRESS PLUGINS

Plugins are tools that can be used to add new features to WordPress.

Installation of the plug-in:
- From the admin panel, click on Plug-ins.
- Scroll down the page to see popular plug-ins in Editors' Choice or Top Free Plug-ins, or use the search box at the top of the Plug-ins screen to find a particular plug-in or feature.
- Click on the name of the plug-in to read information about it: what features it offers, how it works, and how to configure its settings.
- To install the plug-in on the website, click on "Install" and "Activate".

Most plugins are created by developers from around the world. Plug-ins allow you to extend the capabilities of your WordPress website. Before installing a plugin, we recommend that you carry out the checks described below.
- Rating: feedback from customers who have installed this plug-in.
- Latest update: the recent date shows that the plugin is actively maintained and being finalised. If possible, do not use plug-ins that have not been updated for a long time.
- Active installations: The high number of installations indicates the popularity and good support of the plugin.
- Checked on: make sure the plugin is compatible with the version of WordPress you're using. WordPress.com sites automatically use the latest version.

To find out which version of WordPress your site is running, go to Settings -> General, then select View -> Classic View. The WordPress version number will appear in the bottom right corner.

Installing the plug-in using a ZIP file

Some plug-ins do not appear in the search results. In this case you can download the plug-in directly from the developer's website. Usually it is a file in ZIP format[16] , which can be uploaded to the website to install the plug-in.
- On the admin panel, go to the Plug-ins section and click on the

---

[16] 01 A Zip file is an archive that contains files and folders, usually in a compressed form, making them smaller and easier to store or send to other users, for example.

Download button in the top right corner.

- Click to specify the location of the ZIP file on your computer, or drag the file into the box. Do not extract the file before downloading.

Installing the plug-in via SFTP

You can also install plug-ins using Secure File Transfer Protocol (SFTP).

What is SFTP?

This is a way of accessing website files and folders using a software client on a local computer, such as Filezilla[17] .

SFTP stands for Secure File Transfer Protocol or SSH File Transfer Protocol. It is designed as an extension to SSH (Secure SHell) and is secure because it transfers data over a secure SSH channel.

SFTP should not be confused with the FTP file transfer protocol, which allows for similar tasks but is not secure. With SFTP's built-in security features, you can be sure that your files and site are safe.

Some custom plugins and themes may ask you for permission to create folders or add files via SFTP, but the site generally does not require SFTP to work.

Deactivating or removing the plug-in

If the plug-in is no longer needed or if it needs to be temporarily deactivated, deactivate it. Deactivating the plug-in is reversible: the plug-in will remain on your website and can be reactivated if necessary. When the plug-in is reactivated, all its settings and content will be restored.

To deactivate the plug-in:
1. Go to Plug-ins -> Installed plug-ins.
2. Find the plug-in in the list.
3. Press Deactivate.

It is also possible to remove the plug-in from the website without the possibility of restoring it. Option

Uninstall becomes available after deactivating the plug-in as described

---

¹⁷ *01 FileZilla is one of the best free FTP managers to help you download and upload files from FTP servers. The program has a user-friendly and pleasant interface, there are many supported languages and a variety of settings and features. Available for various operating systems, there is a portable version that you can install on a flash drive, and it's also handy for updating files on your hosting service.*

above.

Uninstalling a plug-in will also delete its settings and content, so only uninstall plug-ins that are really unnecessary.

Finding and choosing the best plug-ins

Plug-ins can be extremely useful, so it's important to determine the value and possible problems of each plug-in you add to your site. Just like apps that you install on your phone, choose high-quality, tested and reliable plug-ins.

Before installing the plug-in, pay attention to the following factors

- Availability of the same feature on the site (additional plug-ins can affect the performance of your site, so if the built-in features meet your requirements, we recommend using them);
- Updates and compatibility (Before installing the plug-in, check the date when it was last updated. This information can be found directly under the title on the plug-in page. If the plugin has not been updated for five years, it may mean that its developers have not paid enough attention to it, so it may not work satisfactorily on your site. Look for a plugin that has been updated recently. You can also review the version of WordPress for which the plugin has been tested);
- Popularity (on the plugin page, find the number of active installations. This number indicates how many sites are still using the plugin. If the plugin is popular, it probably means that it is reliable. If the plugin has only been installed a few times, it has not yet been used and tested on many sites. You can also read reviews about the plugin in the WordPress.org plugin repository. Find the desired plugin there and click on the feedback tab to read what other users think of the plugin);
- Support (for a good plugin, an adaptive support service is provided where you can go with any questions or problems related to it.For some plugins, support is provided in the WordPress.org plugin repository. Find the desired plugin there and click its support tab to see if the developer is actively responding to all questions. Other plugins provide a special help centre for their users, with tutorials and/or email addresses where help can be sought. This will be listed in the plugin description. We hope that you will not need to contact the creators of the plugin for help. However, should this happen, remember that you will always get help);
- Evaluation of current plug-ins (the above factors apply equally to plug-ins already running on your website. It is advisable to regularly check the installed plug-ins to remove those that you no longer need. In addition, use the following advice);
- Avoiding identical plug-ins (when looking for a particular feature to add

to your site, you may be tempted to use several different plug-ins. However, as a consequence of installing several plug-ins for the same task, it can be difficult to know which plug-in you like best. Therefore, it is best not to do this. Activate one plug-in, work with it and then deactivate it before activating the next. Once you have found the plug-in that suits you best, delete the other plug-ins);

- Tracking conflicts (a plug-in may not work in combination with other plug-ins. Unless you need to activate several plug-ins at once for simultaneous use, it is advisable to install one plug-in at a time to configure each of them individually. If installing a plug-in leads to undesirable results on your website, you will be able to determine which plug-in caused the problem);
- Update plug-ins (update plug-ins regularly so that only the latest features and protections are available on your website. To check for updates, open the console and go to Plug-ins -> Installed plug-ins);

Resolving problems with plug-ins

Plugins add extra features to your site that are not available by default in the WordPress software. You can find thousands of plugins developed by other users and companies that have opened up access to their plugins to all WordPress users.

Sometimes you may encounter a problem on your website. This guide will help you solve the problem by deactivating plug-ins that may be causing it.

Deactivating plug-ins manually

To troubleshoot problems with third-party plug-ins and themes on your website, follow these steps

- Switch to the default WordPress theme, such as Twenty Twenty, and check if the problem has disappeared.
- If there is no problem, it is related to your topic. In this case you can: a) change the topic; b) contact its author and ask him/her to correct the error.

    - If the problem persists, proceed to the next step.
- Go to Plug-ins -> Installed plug-ins and temporarily deactivate all plug-ins.
- Check if the problem persists. If the error is fixed, it means that deactivated plug-ins were the cause.
- Determine which plug-in is the source of the conflict by activating them

one after the other and checking after each activation. In the case of process-related conflicts, you must repeat the same steps each time.

When you know which plug-in was the source of the problem, you can leave it disconnected and contact the developer to fix the problem.

Plugins and themes not available in the WordPress.org repositories

If you use a plugin or theme that is not available in the WordPress.org repository, updates will not always install automatically. These are usually themes from theme shops such as Envato's Tlieincforesi and plugins purchased directly from the developer's website. Updates for these plug-ins and themes can be manually distributed by developers, or they can provide their own systems for automatic updates. To find out about the update procedure, contact the creators of the plugin or theme directly.

Can an older version of the plugin or theme be installed?

You can install old or outdated versions of plug-ins and themes, but you will need to disable automatic updates to keep them up to date.

REFERENCE LIST

- Grachev A. Creating your own site in WordPress: fast, easy and free [Text]: book. 2nd ed. - St. Petersburg: Peter, 2014.
- Wordpress for Dummies [Electronic resource]: book. - / Course author: Alexander Kadyrov - http://wordpressl.ru
- Savina I.A. Methodology of bibliographical description [Textpractical manual / I.A. Savina. - Moscow: Liberia-Bibinform, 2007. -144 c.
- Levidov, A.M. Literature and Reality / A.M. Levidov. - Leningrad, 1987.-P. 409.

Buy your books fast and straightforward online - at one of world's fastest growing online book stores! Environmentally sound due to Print-on-Demand technologies.

Buy your books online at
www.morebooks.shop

Kaufen Sie Ihre Bücher schnell und unkompliziert online – auf einer der am schnellsten wachsenden Buchhandelsplattformen weltweit! Dank Print-On-Demand umwelt- und ressourcenschonend produzi ert.

Bücher schneller online kaufen
www.morebooks.shop

Printed by Books on Demand GmbH, Norderstedt / Germany